Compliance

A concise guide to the role of the Compliance function in financial services firms

Daniel S Lewis

About the author

Daniel S Lewis is a risk and leadership consultant.

Disclaimer

Table of Contents

1.0 Introduction 6

2.0 What is Compliance? 7
    2.1 Terminology 7
    2.2 Ownership of Compliance 7
    2.3 Three lines of defence 7
    2.4 Independence 8
    2.5 What is Conduct Risk? 9
    2.6 Regulatory Risk vs. Conduct Risk 9
    2.7 'Compliance 1.0' vs. ' Compliance 2.0' 10

3.0 Role and activities of the Compliance function 12
    3.1 Advisory/line of business Compliance 13
    3.2 Regulatory Management/Country Compliance 13
    3.3 Trade Surveillance 13
    3.4 Communications Monitoring 15
    3.5 Risk Assessment 15
    3.6 Compliance Review 16
    3.7 Personal Account Dealing ('PAD') 17
    3.8 Outside business interests 17
    3.9 Gifts & Entertainment 17
    3.10 Employee Licensing 18
    3.11 Transaction Reporting 18
    3.12 Investigations 18
    3.13 Compliance Policy 19
    3.14 Education & Training 19
    3.15 Investment Guidelines Compliance 20
    3.16 Shareholder Reporting/Disclosure of Interest 20
    3.17 Financial Crime Compliance 20
    3.18 Control Room 22
    3.19 Research Compliance 23
    3.20 Data Protection ('DP') 23
    3.21 Banking Secrecy 23
    3.22 'Private-side Compliance' 24
    3.23 Cross-border Compliance 25
    3.24 Whistleblowing 25

4.0 Skills of the Effective Compliance Professional.........26

5.0 Ethics, Culture, and Compliance 28

6.0 Some Opportunities & Challenges....................................30
    6.1 'Accepted' vs. 'acceptable' practices....................................30
    6.2 Better conduct – self-initiated or regulator-initiated?.30
    6.3 Inherent risk in a 'Trust & Verify' model 31
    6.4 Increasing the amount of 'Forced Compliance'...............31
    6.5 Measuring risk 31
    6.6 Big data & technology 32
    6.7 Controlling the known vs. the unknown 32
    6.8 Moving operational processes to Operations.................33
    6.9 Second line testing – ineffective and duplicative 33
    6.10 Talent..33
    6.11 The Culture Delusion..33
    6.12 Independence 34

A final word...35

1.0 Introduction

Compliance continues to be an increasingly important requirement in the financial services industry.

In recent years, Compliance failures have cost financial services firms billions in regulatory fines and related costs. The Conduct Costs Project[1], a London School of Economics initiative, calculates that banks have borne costs related to conduct failings in excess of GBP 200bn in the period 2010-2014. This is an enormous sum of money, particularly at a time when many financial services firms continue to struggle in the post-financial crisis era, both in adjusting to challenging business conditions, and in adjusting to more onerous capital requirements.

In addition to the financial costs of misconduct, there are often other non-financial costs to be borne in the form of reputational damage, and ruined careers. It's often not just the individual directly involved in the misconduct who is punished, but also the people responsible for supervising and controlling them. This human impact is sometimes less apparent in the reporting of enforcement action taken by regulatory authorities.

While the level of regulatory financial penalties for firms has reached record highs, many countries are now taking steps to increase the ability of regulators to take direct action against individuals involved in compliance and conduct failings.

---

[1] http://conductcosts.ccpresearchfoundation.com/conduct-costs-results

2.0 What is Compliance?

2.1 Terminology

Compliance is the process of identifying and managing the regulatory and conduct risks that a firm is exposed to. Regulatory and conduct risks arise both from exposure to external requirements, such as the rules applied by regulators, and internal requirements, such as the policies and procedures that have been established and put in place by a firm.

In this book, the term 'Compliance' should be taken to refer to both regulatory and conduct matters. The term 'standards' is used to refer to external and internal requirements that staff and firms are required to follow.

As a topic, Compliance is often bundled with Ethics in the discourse that takes place in the media and in other forums. Whether one takes a narrow view or a broad view of Compliance, there is arguably a strong relationship between Compliance and Ethics. However, Compliance and Ethics are not the same, and this is touched on further in Chapter 5.

2.2 Ownership of Compliance

The Board of Directors of a firm is ultimately responsible for overseeing the management of compliance risk. The Board, or a sub-committee, should periodically review the extent to which the firm is managing compliance risk effectively.

The firm's senior management are responsible for the day-to-day management of compliance risk. Practically, senior management will share this responsibility across the 'three lines of defence'.

2.3 Three lines of defence

Most firms take a 'three lines of defence' approach to the management of compliance risk.

The first line of defence consists of the business and front-line staff. The first line has primary responsibility for day-to-day risk management, and will ultimately bear the consequences of any failures to manage risk effectively.

The second line of defence is Compliance and other risk management functions. Second line functions assist in determining risk capacity, risk appetite, and frameworks for managing risk.

The third line of defence is Audit, and the Board of Directors. The Board sets risk appetite and provides oversight. Audit, both in its internal and external forms, provides independent and objective assurance on the overall effectiveness of the risk governance framework.

2.4 Independence

The Compliance function must be independent of the business in order for it to operate effectively. There are four elements to independence, as below.

First, the Compliance function should have formal organisational status within the firm.

Second, a Head of Compliance should be in place that has overall responsibility for coordinating the management of Compliance risk.

Third, staff in the Compliance function should not be placed in a position where there is a possible conflict of interest between their Compliance responsibilities and any other responsibilities they may have.

Fourth, staff in the Compliance function should have access to the information and personnel necessary to carry out their responsibilities.

The maintenance and development of the independence of the Compliance function continues to pose challenges for

Compliance professionals, and this is touched on further in Chapter 6.

2.5 What is Conduct Risk?

The term 'Conduct Risk' has emerged following incidents of misconduct in financial firms in recent years, such as LIBOR manipulation and the mis-selling of payment protection insurance. However, there is nothing new about the concept of risk due to misconduct.

Conduct risk is simply the risk that the business, or the staff within the business, fail to act in an appropriate way on behalf of the firm. In practice, this means adhering to internal and external requirements, and behaving in a way that is consistent with fair treatment of clients, and fair treatment of other participants in financial markets.

And while the term 'Conduct Risk' does not describe anything new, increasing use of this term has signalled a change in the emphasis now given to the management of regulatory and conduct risks in firms.

2.6 Regulatory Risk vs. Conduct Risk

Regulatory Risk is the risk of financial loss, reputational harm, or constraints, being imposed on a firm arising from a failure to adequately adhere to the requirements of regulators and/or legislation governing financial services matters.

As explained above, Conduct Risk involves a broader view of risk because conduct failures can arise in circumstances that are not directly or apparently governed by regulatory rules or laws, such as in the case of the LIBOR and FX enforcement actions taken by US and UK regulators in recent years. While the LIBOR and FX issues involved activities that were technically not regulated in rulebooks, regulators took action under regulatory principles and under other legislation e.g. fraud laws.

The distinction between Regulatory Risk and Conduct Risk doesn't practically need to arise if a broad view of compliance risk in financial services firms is taken. However, this distinction can continue to legitimately be made, and some people still take a narrow view of compliance risks – focusing on regulatory compliance and the requirements of regulators alone, rather than considering compliance risk more broadly. This is a high-risk strategy – while compliance with rules and explicit requirements is obviously a necessary condition for effective compliance, it is not a sufficient one.

2.7 'Compliance 1.0' vs. ' Compliance 2.0'

Some compliance professionals and writers on Compliance refer to 'Compliance 2.0', as (by implication) distinct from 'Compliance 1.0'. What are they referring to?

Following the financial crisis, a paradigm shift in many firms' approach to compliance occurred – a shift to what some would describe as Compliance 2.0. Three significant developments in Compliance have resulted in the Compliance 2.0 descriptor.

First, Compliance has become a more independent function at many firms with a direct reporting line into the Chief Executive or Head of Risk. Previously, many Compliance functions were adjuncts of the Legal function, organisationally designated as 'Legal & Compliance'. Compliance was usually the junior partner in these combinations. As the role of Compliance became more concerned with control and the management of risk, it became increasingly less appropriate to bundle compliance and legal activities together. Consequently, many 'Legal & Compliance' functions have been split, leaving Compliance as a stand-alone function.

Second, Compliance 1.0 may be described as the period during which the business failed to take sufficient ownership of compliance risks, relying too much on the Compliance function to manage compliance risk. The first line of defence had, it is argued, in effect outsourced its role to the second line. An example of this is the numerous different types of approvals that the business would seek from, and be given by, Compliance functions. Instead of making appropriate judgements for itself, too many first line business and compliance risk management decisions were delegated to Compliance. So Compliance 2.0 is the result of a recalibration of first and second line responsibilities, where the business has taken better ownership of its first line risk management role.

Third, Compliance 1.0 was characterised by the Compliance function often having to work too hard to persuade the business of the importance of managing compliance risk effectively. Compliance 2.0 therefore represents a 'post-persuasion' era, where the business understands, and has bought in to, its compliance risk management role.

3.0 Role and activities of the Compliance function

In this Chapter I consider the role and activities of the Compliance function in detail. In larger firms, dedicated staff or teams will typically be responsible for these activities. In smaller firms, Compliance staff may be responsible for one or more of these activities.

The Compliance function is responsible for identifying and managing, from a second line of defence perspective, the compliance risks that the business is exposed to. The Compliance function carries out activities under the following main headings in order to achieve this.

Guidance & advice: providing guidance to the business on internal and external standards; establishing written guidance to staff on the appropriate implementation of laws and regulations ('external standards') and developing internal standards in the form of policies and procedures, compliance manuals, and codes of conduct.

Education: educating staff on compliance issues, and responding to queries on compliance matters made by staff.

Identification, measurement, and assessment of compliance risk: operating risk assessment programmes to assess and measure risk.

Monitoring, testing, and reporting: monitoring and testing for adherence to internal and external standards.

Regulatory responsibilities and regulatory liaison: liaising with relevant regulatory authorities.

These activities are considered in more detail below. For ease of description, the activities are described as being performed by a dedicated function.

3.1 Advisory/line of business Compliance

This activity involves a combination of advising and guiding the business on the day-to-day management of compliance risk, and providing support to the business on relevant internal & external standards.

Individuals performing this role may also be responsible for preparing and delivering compliance training, including tailor-made training for specific business areas where required.

Evaluation of proposals for new business activities, and considering the compliance implications and risks therein, would also fall under the 'advisory' category.

3.2 Regulatory Management/Country Compliance

Regulatory management activity typically involves liaising with external regulators, and ensuring that the firm is legally authorised to conduct its activities.

Regulators often submit requests to firms for information e.g. the number of clients engaging in a certain type of activity, the numbers of transactions completed in a certain instrument etc. Also, regulators will undertake inspection visits from time-to-time. These matters would be dealt with and coordinated under Regulatory Management activities.

Firms with offices in multiple jurisdictions may have additional staff devoted to regulatory management for the relevant countries – such staff may be referred to as members of a 'Country Compliance' function.

3.3 Trade Surveillance

The purpose of trade surveillance activity is to identify unusual or suspicious transactions that may be inappropriate with respect to compliance standards, or market practices generally. Trade surveillance systems are used to analyse transactions in order to identify possibly suspicious transactions which are then investigated by Compliance staff.

Examples of the type of activity targeted by trade surveillance programmes include the following.

Non-market price transactions. Trades executed at prices which are not consistent with market prices or which are inconsistent with trades in the market at that time in the relevant size.

Spoofing and layering. Placing of artificial orders that are cancelled without being executed in an attempt to impact the perceived demand or liquidity for an instrument and hence the market price.

Best execution. Trades executed at prices that do not meet the criteria established for best execution when compared to available benchmark prices or rolling average of benchmark prices.

Front-running of clients. Trading ahead of orders (or in parallel with orders) that have been given to a firm to execute in order to take advantage of anticipated price movements to either make a profit or avoid a loss.

Abusive squeeze. Trades executed to manipulate the price of an instrument with the intention of distorting the price at which others have to deliver, take delivery, or defer delivery to meet their obligations.

Front-running the market. Trading ahead of a market announcement of price sensitive information either in the instrument affected or an associated derivative to take advantage of anticipated price movements to either make a profit or avoid a loss.

Wash trades. Trades executed with no obvious change in beneficial ownership or for no obvious economic benefit, but done purely to artificially impact perceived market demand or market liquidity.

Unusual transactions. Trades that have unusual features that could indicate unauthorised or manipulative behaviour e.g. restructured trades that could help clients to window-dress their own performance.

Most trade surveillance performed by Compliance functions is post-trade surveillance. However, firms are increasingly considering whether and how pre-trade surveillance routines may be effective e.g. preventing inappropriate trades being executed in the first place by applying measures to trading systems.

3.4 Communications Monitoring

Audio and electronic communications monitoring is an activity that has seen significant expansion in recent years. The purpose of this monitoring is to identify communications that might indicate inappropriate behaviour by front line staff involving clients, or other market participants.

Many firms have overhauled their communications monitoring practices following the LIBOR and FX scandals, which made infamous certain examples of electronic messages sent between traders who were manipulating interest rate benchmark submissions and foreign exchange prices.

3.5 Risk Assessment

Compliance Risk Assessment ('CRA') work is an important part of ensuring a robust compliance programme. CRA work provides insights into the risk profile of the firm and into the strength of the control environment. It also enables assessment of compliance risks arising from business activities and the strength of the infrastructure to mitigate those risks. The results of CRA work should drive areas of focus for the compliance programme (e.g. monitoring and testing) and can also drive ongoing enhancement of the overall compliance framework.

Regulators expect CRA work to be a foundation of the ongoing management and enhancement of compliance programmes. Compliance management should be able to articulate the compliance risk profile of the business generally, and for specific areas of the business. The CRA also supports reporting to the Chief Executive and the Board.

Obviously, the larger and more diverse the business, the more complex CRA will be. Further complexity arises if business is undertaken in multiple jurisdictions – in such cases firms will decide whether to whether to adopt a global or regional approach to CRA. A global approach may pose challenges in capturing jurisdictional aspects of risk – whether due to the particular nature of the business in that jurisdiction and/or due to local regulatory or legal requirements. Regulatory requirements specific to individual jurisdictions should obviously be reflected in the CRA.

An effective CRA process should have a robust methodology for measuring and categorising risk, and should not be over-reliant on anecdotal views or gut feeling. While CRA work should take account of historical issues, it should not be over-weighted to known issues. Known issues should already be the subjects of remediation – risk is about uncertainty.

It is important that CRA outputs remain useful and that they influence decision-making. CRA work that merely paints a picture, and that does not drive action, is a failure.

3.6 Compliance Review

In addition to trade and communications surveillance activities, many firms have a compliance testing team that resembles an internal audit function. Firms use different labels such as Compliance Review, Compliance Risk Review, Compliance Testing, and Compliance Desk Review etc.

The purpose of compliance review activity is to test for compliance in the business. A combined 'vertical' and or 'horizontal' approach to testing is common. Vertical testing involves testing discrete areas of the business for broad adherence to compliance requirements – this type of testing is broad in scope and narrow in depth. Horizontal or thematic testing takes a particular compliance requirement and tests it across the business or across a number of business areas – so this testing is narrow in scope and deep in depth.

The findings and recommendations arising from compliance review work are presented to management in a similar way that an Internal Audit function would. Findings of review work should also be used to inform and update the CRA.

3.7 Personal Account Dealing ('PAD')

Personal investment or personal account dealing activity undertaken privately by employees can conflict with the interests of the firm, or with clients. For example, an employee might front-run a client order by privately dealing for himself or herself beforehand. Personal investment activity is therefore governed by policies & procedures. These standards typically require pre-approval for employee investments, and apply requirements such as minimum holding periods. Such standards would also usually apply to the spouse/partner and children of the employee.

3.8 Outside business interests

Personal and private business interests of employees can also lead to conflicts with their firm or with clients, and this is therefore governed by standards. For example, the operation of an investment firm established privately by an employee could conflict with the interests of the firm employing them.

3.9 Gifts & Entertainment

The provision or receipt of gifts and entertainment ('G&E') by or from employees, to or from clients, can also cause conflicts, and therefore controls are required. For example, a gift provided to the employee of a client could inappropriately induce that employee to deal with the firm that provided the gift, regardless of whether this is in the employing client's interest or not.

3.10 Employee Licensing

Some jurisdictions require employees undertaking investment activity to be licensed by, or registered with, a regulator. Compliance is often responsible for licensing new staff, unlicensing former staff, and updating the static details of ongoing licensed staff.

3.11 Transaction Reporting

Some jurisdictions require certain transactions to be reported to a regulator for the purpose of monitoring and overseeing market integrity. Within a firm, this activity will usually be owned and executed by the Operations function. This is an activity that Compliance should keep in view in its second line role e.g. periodic compliance testing could be carried out to test that the data reported is complete and accurate.

3.12 Investigations

Investigative activity is often required in financial firms when actual or suspected cases of misconduct arise. Investigations may be carried out by the Compliance function, and may be carried out jointly with Legal staff, in order to preserve legal privilege and to ensure that the interests of the firm are otherwise protected through the undertaking of the investigation in an appropriate manner.

When problems are found, root causes should be identified quickly and any necessary remedial action (e.g. addressing control deficiencies) should be taken without delay. Some firms have been criticised by regulators in the past for waiting until the conclusion of an investigation to take action, despite required remedies becoming apparent early on.

3.13 Compliance Policy

Compliance policies are required to set out written standards for a firm on regulatory and conduct matters. Policies are generally high-level documents – different parts of a business may need local procedures to govern how policies are applied to that business in practice.

Regulatory change matters will usually be analysed by staff responsible for Compliance policy, who will propose amendments to the relevant polices as appropriate.

3.14 Education & Training

Preparing and delivering education and training is an important element of a Compliance programme. Training is delivered to refresh on existing topics, and to educate on developments in practices and standards. Training may be provided online or in person.

Online training is efficient in its ability to provide mass training cheaply. However, online training on 'dry' topics can be uninteresting for the recipients and many people may simply click through the training. Also, online training may not be suitable for more complex subjects. It is difficult to establish the effectiveness of online training. Modules may end with a test that must be passed. Passed tests can indicate that recipients have gained knowledge, however this may be forgotten soon after the test. Or passed tests can simply be gamed or passed with enough attempts.

In-person training is generally more effective than online training, provided the trainer has sufficient competence in the subject matter and sufficient ability to communicate it. This effectiveness comes at a price, however. In-person training can be a relatively labour-intensive activity for Compliance staff given the number of sessions usually required to deliver it to all recipients. It is also potentially disruptive to the business to have too many staff attending a particular training session at any one time.

3.15 Investment Guidelines Compliance

In businesses involving investment management or fund management activities, monitoring compliance with investment guidelines is required to ensure that management of client assets is done in accordance with the stated investment guidelines and restrictions.

3.16 Shareholder Reporting/Disclosure of Interest

Shareholder reporting, or disclosure of interest, is the activity of discharging obligations to report and disclose aggregated shareholdings across a firm in accordance with regulatory and legal requirements in all relevant jurisdictions. This includes reporting on any short positions that are required to be disclosed under short-selling rules.

3.17 Financial Crime Compliance

The prevention and detection of financial crime, particularly money laundering, has been a high priority for financial regulators for more than two decades. Tackling financial crime continues to be a priority for regulators, not least since the September 2011 attacks, and given the continuing risks of global terrorism.

Financial crime compliance can be divided into several areas as below.

Anti-Money Laundering ('AML') & Combating the Financing of Terrorism ('CFT')

Money laundering is the process by which the proceeds of crime are brought into the financial system in order to conceal the illegal origin of the funds. Such funds may be obtained through organised crime, drug trafficking, or other criminal activity. Concealing the origin of the proceeds of crime ('laundering') allows criminals to use this money as though it was legitimate money in the financial system. Terrorists and terrorist organisations also employ techniques to hide and disguise money.

Governments around the world recognise the dangers that money laundering and terrorist financing pose to their economic and political systems, and a large body of legislation and regulations has grown up around AML and CFT.

The role of Compliance is to develop and execute an AML/CFT programme to ensure that an appropriate control and risk management framework is in place. This would include developing policies and procedures that are designed to deter and detect money laundering and terrorist financing, including appropriate 'Know Your Client' requirements (ensuring that only legitimate clients are taken on and that the source of their funds is legitimate), developing and delivering training, supporting the business on specific queries and scenarios, and ensuring independent audits of the programme.

Sanctions Compliance

Compliance with economic sanctions imposed by governments on individuals, institutions, and nation states is a significant area of compliance work for many financial firms. The USA, European Union, and United Nations, maintain separate sanctions lists, adding to the complexities of compliance with sanctions.

This is an area that firms have had to invest more resources in to ensure they are able to comply. Particular compliance work that would support compliance with sanctions includes developing and implementing control processes for sanctions compliance, and providing advice and guidance to the business and other functions on managing the risks involved.

Anti-Bribery & Corruption ('ABC')

The enforcement of anti-bribery and corruption laws continues to be a focus area for governments and regulators around the world. Bribery is the practice of offering something, usually money, in order to facilitate a transaction, or to gain an unfair advantage. Corruption is an abuse of a position of trust in relation to an unfair advantage.

The role of Compliance in relation to ABC includes providing technical advice and support to the business in order to ensure compliance with relevant internal and external requirements.

Market Abuse

Market abuse refers to non-compliant and/or illegal activity that results in disadvantage or detriment to other users of financial markets. Market abuse is usually split into two categories – misuse of information and market manipulation.

Misuse of information includes insider dealing i.e. where non-public price-sensitive information is used to make a profit or avoid a loss. Market manipulation includes activities such as trading in an instrument merely to position or manipulate its price, and giving a false impression of the demand of supply or an instrument (e.g. through inappropriate use of orders).

The role of Compliance in relation to market abuse includes providing technical advice and support to the business in order to support compliance with relevant internal and external standards and requirements. This is in addition to the activities performed under the heading of Trade Surveillance.

3.18 Control Room

The Control Room is a function found in investment bank Compliance functions. Control rooms provide a central hub through which conflicts of interest across different areas of the business can be identified, recorded, and managed. Another key role that the control room performs is to support the business in controlling the flow of confidential and inside information.

3.19 Research Compliance

Research compliance is a relatively specialised activity found in firms that publish research on issuers of securities, or on interest rate or foreign exchange markets.

Regulatory rules on research require that it be clear, fair, and represent a true opinion objectively held by the firm.

Conflicts of interest can arise in relation to research, as exposed by the Spitzer-led investigations in the early 2000's. Eliot Spitzer, New York State Attorney General at the time, determined that research analysts for certain investment firms wrote biased research in favour of investment banking corporate clients instead of providing objective and independent analysis to investors. The resulting 'Global Research Settlement' with investment firms changed the way conflicts of interest in research are managed around the world.

3.20 Data Protection ('DP')

Various jurisdictions have DP laws comprising rules governing the collection, use, disclosure, and care, of personal data. Such laws recognise the rights of individuals to protect their personal data, including rights of access and correction, and the needs of organisations to collect, use, or disclose, personal data for legitimate and reasonable purposes.

The role of Compliance with respect to DP is to ensure that appropriate policies and arrangements are in place, and to be a subject matter expert on DP such as to field queries on the practical application of DP requirements in particular scenarios.

3.21 Banking Secrecy

Certain jurisdictions have banking secrecy rules that forbid the disclosure of the identity and transactions of clients to third parties unless the consent of the client has been obtained. Secrecy laws can also restrict disclosure within firms by forbidding disclosure to employees of the firm outside of the secrecy jurisdiction.

Similarly for DP, the role of Compliance here is to ensure that appropriate policies are in place, and to be a subject matter expert on the application of secrecy requirements in practice.

3.22 'Private-side Compliance'

Some firms, especially investment banks, have Chinese walls that divide the business into 'public-side' and 'private-side'.

Public-side businesses in such firms typically comprise sales and trading activities e.g. market-making and executing orders in tradable financial instruments such as stocks and bonds.

Private-side businesses in such firms involve advising on mergers & acquisitions, lending, and arranging the issuance of stocks and bonds for companies. Private-side activities often involve handling of 'inside information' i.e. confidential unpublished information that investors in a company's stocks or bonds would deem relevant to their trading decisions.

Chinese walls are the set of physical and administrative arrangements that separate public-side and private-side staff, so that public-side staff can conduct markets activities while inside information is held elsewhere in the firm. Dealing with issues that can arise around practical application of Chinese walls is one area of focus in private-side compliance work.

Conflicts of interest between the firm and a client, or between clients, can also arise in private-side businesses and this is another matter that would be supported under private-side compliance activity.

Another area requiring Compliance support is adherence to takeover rules. Several jurisdictions require adherence to detailed requirements in takeover situations, especially hostile takeovers, and this is another source of private-side compliance work.

3.23 Cross-border Compliance

Cross-border compliance is concerned with ensuring that business carried out with clients located in other jurisdictions is permitted and/or does not contradict any licensing requirements of the client's jurisdiction. For example, unlicensed investment activity by firms located outside the USA with clients located in the USA may only be done in adherence with the '15a-6' exemption.

Many firms will have a set of guidance and procedures for each country that they provide cross-border services into. Such procedures would cover visits by staff to those countries, as well as activity performed 'remotely' into such countries e.g. by telephone, by email etc.

3.24 Whistleblowing

A whistleblower is an employee that reports an employer's misconduct. Many jurisdictions have laws that protect whistleblowers from being dismissed or mistreated for reporting misconduct.

Some firms assign responsibility for investigating reported Whistleblowing to the Compliance function. When individual employees who qualify as whistleblowers raise issues, it's important that, as well as investigating the substance of the allegations, that a firm proceeds carefully to ensure that no mistreatment of the whistleblower occurs.

The availability of incentives for whistleblowers, particularly in the USA, may encourage more whistleblowing in the future, adding to the compliance burden for firms. In the USA, the Securities and Exchange Commission ('SEC') is authorised to provide monetary awards to whistleblowers who produce 'high-quality original information' that leads to enforcement action. Whistleblowers can be eligible to receive awards ranging between 10% and 30% of fines imposed.

4.0 Skills of the Effective Compliance Professional

The Compliance profession is diverse. Many Compliance staff have backgrounds as lawyers, accountants, or a background in the business. There is no simple model of a typical Compliance professional.

The junior ranks of Compliance staff are generally mainly occupied with mastering the technical aspects of their roles – such as developing their knowledge of compliance standards and applying them in practice to the responsibilities assigned to them.

The middle and senior ranks of compliance professionals, having mastered technical basics, will be more focused (from a skills development perspective) on developing more advanced approaches to compliance risk management. They will also be focused on developing their management skills, particularly in respect of people management, project management, relationship management, and conflict resolution.

The average job specification for a Compliance professional will set out general criteria as follows. Depending on the nature and seniority of the role, some criteria (and the strength of ability in them) will be obviously be more important than others.

Business knowledge: understanding and knowledge of the business in general, and products in particular.

Compliance knowledge: understanding and knowledge of the compliance standards that apply to the business.

Practical experience: ability to apply knowledge of compliance standards to the business, and evaluate and analyse compliance risk in that context.

Relationship handling skills: ability to manage relationships with the businesses at all levels, including senior management; ability to build and maintain strong working relationships with stakeholders and using them to achieve Compliance objectives; ability to manage relationships with regulators.

Judgement: ability to 'think on feet', often providing real-time advice and guidance under time pressure and in high profile situations.

Collaboration: ability to work as part of real and virtual teams.

Proactivness: ability to take initiative and act proactively; proactiveness in the identification of new/changing compliance risk, and in the identification and exploitation of opportunities to improve the management of compliance risk.

Communication skills: ability to make and present, orally and in writing, persuasive arguments to support views and guidance given to the business and other functions.

Analytical skills: ability to analyse information and processes in light of internal and external standards.

5.0 Ethics, Culture, and Compliance

An ethical culture is often described as one where people do the right thing without being told to.

In the corporate environment, many people think of ethics as a question of personal conscience. They may be quick to describe any misconduct as an isolated incident – the work of 'one bad apple in the barrel' perhaps. The idea that a firm could also be responsible for its employees' misconduct can be difficult for such people to come to terms with.

The causes of misconduct can rarely be attributed in isolation to the flaws and shortcomings of a single individual. Misconduct, and unethical practices, usually involves the cooperation of others, whether active or passive.

Ethics is probably therefore as much of a management issue as a personal one. Management is responsible for providing appropriate leadership, and maintaining systems, such as to facilitate ethical conduct.

'Culture' is a term often referred to by firms and the financial industry. The industry has spoken about culture for many years, and culture is usually cited as an area for improvement when there are firm and industry-wide conduct failings. Following such failings, reassurances may be given by firms to regulators and politicians that improvements in culture have subsequently been achieved.

However, conduct failings continue to occur despite reassurances that significant improvements in culture have been made. So why are some people convinced that improvements in culture will provide a powerful panacea?

Obviously, culture has a part to play in any control environment. The more disposed that people are to behaving ethically and in adherence with a firm's values, the less likely that incidences of misconduct will occur. However, improvements in ethical culture are unlikely to be the panacea that many hold it up to be. The importance of a robust and developing control environment that retains pace with the business should, therefore, not be understated.

'Physician, heal thyself'. Compliance and risk management professionals should tread carefully when preaching ethics and values to the business. While Compliance staff will have more in-depth knowledge of regulatory and conduct compliance matters than the business, there is no evidence to suggest that the average Compliance staffer is any more ethical, or behaves with greater integrity, than the average business person. A recent news story –'Cyber shock: Compliance staff perhaps the most likely to steal insider data[2]' – may be of interest.

---

[2] http://www.cityam.com/238286/cyber-shock-Compliance-staff-perhaps-the-most-likely-to-steal-insider-data

6.0 Some Opportunities & Challenges

As the role of Compliance shifts towards that of a risk management function, the challenges for the Compliance function of the future will continue to be significant. Effective risk management depends on the identification of new risks, while sustaining and improving the management of existing risks. In this chapter, I offer some thoughts on several opportunities and challenges facing the Compliance function.

6.1 'Accepted' vs. 'acceptable' practices

One of the most common responses heard by Compliance professionals when they challenge or question business practices is 'well, everyone does it that way'. While this is often true, it obviously does not mean it is right. Compliance professionals, particularly junior ones, can also fall into this mindset, and can struggle to challenge it. If there is a reasonable question mark over the appropriateness of a certain practice, the answer that it is 'market practice' is not sufficient by itself, and the matter should not be left there. This is easier said than done.

6.2 Better conduct – self-initiated or regulator-initiated?

Firms need to decide if they are going to proactively improve conduct risk management by seeking opportunities to do so, or whether they prefer not to risk loss of competitive advantage by restricting or ceasing questionable practices before their competitors do. While firms will state publicly that they are proactive on conduct risk management, the experience of past failures does not bear this out. It remains to be seen whether a new approach will emerge. Given the enormous sums borne by firms relating to conduct issues, it makes economic sense for firms and the industry to proactively "heal itself" on an ongoing basis, rather than wait for punishment from regulators as a catalyst for action.

6.3 Inherent risk in a 'Trust & Verify' model

In most financial firms, the control environment is heavily dependent on humans doing the right thing. For example, staff in the business are trusted to sell the right products to the right clients, and to enter the true details of transactions into systems. There is relatively little 'forced Compliance' in financial services. Yes, there is an increasing amount of 'verification' control work being performed, and this is necessary because of the amount of trust placed in staff, and the scope for human error. However, recent scandals, including rogue trading, resulting in losses or fines of billions of dollars for banks, show just how vulnerable firms still are to misconduct, or mistakes, committed by staff in the business.

6.4 Increasing the amount of 'Forced Compliance'

Forced compliance is about reducing the extent to which there is reliance on trust, and reliance on humans getting things right, by redesigning processes and adding more information technology to them. For example, if a transaction can only be executed electronically if certain conditions are present (e.g. permission to trade) and if the transaction is automatically processed after execution without the possibility, or need, for human intervention, this would be a process that you could describe as having compliance forced into it. Forced compliance processes are obviously much less risky than processes that depend on human accuracy and integrity. The increasing extent to which technology is changing processes in financial services businesses therefore offers opportunities to force more compliance into such processes.

6.5 Measuring risk

While most Compliance functions will have some type of Compliance Risk Assessment programme, many such programmes struggle to be effective. Many CRA programmes are merely 'picture-painting' exercises that are done without a robust methodology, relying on the gut feeling and recent experiences of Compliance staff alone. They can also be backward-looking – reflecting historical issues that may have no relevance to an assessment of current or future risk. Effective CRA programmes should also drive the allocation of Compliance resources e.g. focus areas for compliance testing, but many do not. Most firms will need to make significant improvements to their CRA programme in order for Compliance to become an effective risk management function.

6.6 Big data & technology

Traditional compliance surveillance and testing activities generally struggle to be effective. They are usually carried out as post-trade activities designed to find problems after they have occurred. Increasing use of 'big data' can allow firms to monitor for red flags and inappropriate behaviour before serious problems occur. Using algorithms to triangulate data, and analysing patterns in data, can identify leads for further investigation. Some firms compare profitability levels of business staff against other metrics to look for outliers e.g. if one person makes the same number of phone calls as another person, but sells twice as much, why is that? Is it because of legitimate factors (maybe they are just a better salesperson), or because of potentially illegitimate factors, such as mis-selling? So the increasing availability of data, and the technology to analyse it, presents a substantial opportunity for Compliance functions.

6.7 Controlling the known vs. the unknown

While many firms have made significant additional investment into their Compliance functions, most of this investment is directed at controlling risks that are already known. Compliance staff continue to be criticised by regulators for being insufficiently intellectually curious. More proactive risk identification, and improvement of the management of existing risks, is therefore required.

6.8 Moving operational processes to Operations

Compliance functions usually run operational processes, such as processing information relating to personal account dealing, gifts & entertainment, and licensing. These activities belong more in an operations function and less in a risk management function. Removing these activities should allow the Compliance function to focus on risk management, rather than process management.

6.9 Second line testing – ineffective and duplicative

Much of what Compliance does under the banner of 'testing' is duplicative, or complementary to, work done by the Internal Audit function. Also, Compliance testing teams often struggle to be effective. Some Compliance functions have different models, or are not even clear about which model they are following in respect of the skills they seek in their testing staff. Some want people with strong Compliance skills that know something about testing, and some want people with strong testing skills that know something about Compliance. It may be advisable to transfer this testing work to professionals in the Internal Audit function. This would enable Compliance to focus on its role as a risk management function, leaving assurance gathering activities to be done by auditing experts.

6.10 Talent

The Compliance profession is experiencing a skills shortage. While there have been many new entrants to the profession at the junior levels, it will obviously take time for these staff to develop in seniority. Firms should ensure that they are investing sufficient management time, and money, into the development of their juniors.

6.11 The Culture Delusion

As mentioned in Chapter 5, financial services firms have talked about making improvements in culture for decades and, while the industry certainly appears to have renewed its efforts in this area, it remains to be seen whether an improved industry culture can be achieved, and demonstrated, in the form of fewer cases of widespread misconduct in the future. Driving improvements in culture is primarily a matter for the business, and not for Compliance. For these reasons, Compliance professionals should resist being drawn too much into work involving culture, and instead focus on making improvements in compliance risk management.

6.12 Independence

Compliance functions are still struggling to influence and control the business effectively, as shown by recent industry scandals. Greater operational independence for Compliance is required if it is to secure a role as an effective risk management function. The business still tends to significantly influence Compliance hiring, promotion, and compensation decisions. This weakens the independence of the Compliance function and weakens the appetite of Compliance staff to challenge the business. Some firms may decide to build greater independence into their Compliance functions by having the Head of Compliance report to a non-executive member of the Board.

A final word

Thanks for reading this book.

If you found it useful, I'd be really grateful if you could please leave me a review on Amazon.

It should only take a minute and you don't have to use your real name.

Every review means a lot to me.

Thanks for your support!

Daniel

www.ingramcontent.com/pod-product-compliance
Lightning Source LLC
Chambersburg PA
CBHW070424190526
45169CB00003B/1406